MY GRANDMA AND OTHER POETRY

ADITYA KUMAR PANDA

ISBN 979-888555691-0

Contents

Preface

This is a book of poetry titled My Grandma and Other Poetry. My Grandma is the first poetry and my grandma and my daughter's gannies are the harbinger of this little book of poetry. Other poems are about existence, modernity and impact of technology on life style and present-day affairs. I could not separate these from my thoughts on grandmaa because all these exist in my experience in a time as a whole.

Aditya Kumar Panda
NTM, CIIL, Mysore-570006
Mob: 9886705545

Prologue

MaaMaa, aimaa, daadimaa-these are the words we use while referring to our grandmother or granny in Odia. Grandmother occupies a significant role in our lives. She becomes our friend-philosopher-guide and cheerleader, importantly our famous heart touching storyteller. The most memorable act that she does is the storytelling. She is our first storyteller. These stories revolve around the Ramayana, the Mahabharata, other mythologies, local folklores and legends. This is a means, she uses to spend time with us, to divert our attention, to educate us, to encourage us for doing good things, to prevent us from immoral unruly things. Don't you think that this act of our granny contributes to the development of our social moral aesthetical beings? Yes, it does. Her acts, stories and habits get imprinted in our minds and hearts. I could summarize these transactions as follows which may not be applicable for all:

Freedom means granny, restriction means parents

Heart means granny, mind means parents

Acceptance means granny, denial means parents

Whatever it may be! Every child loves her/his granny. I always think about granny and it has given me lot of thoughts that I have woven my thoughts in the form of poetry. The first poetry in this anthology is My Grandma. This anthology of poetry also has poetry that depicts the impact of modernity, questions of self and existence. But the poetry Grandma inspire all these depictions.

Hope the readers will enjoy reading these poems and these will renew their thoughts about granny-grandmaa-grandmother. I should mention here that grandma is our huge cultural heritage. The grandma, who has become my source of morality and dos and don'ts and the source of this little book, is a prototype who can be seen in your house or in your neighbour's house or in your relative's house. She has become an institution-an agent of a culture/society. I could remember how grandmothers whom I have seen, were able to recite Odia proverbs/idioms so fluently and able to describe to the listeners with examples from mythologies. These proverbs were not only from mythological books but also from oral traditions which have so many unrecorded proverbs and idioms. I could translate one of these proverbs here:

House says go go

Farm says come come

Its meaning:

I don't have more time in this world. My time is over. My life activities at my home are getting over and my life is coming to an end, the farm land (refers to burial ground) is calling me means I will be a part of the dust soon (will pass away soon).

Aditya Kumar Panda

Keshaipali, 6th January, 2022

1. My Grandma

I could see a star hereafter
She was telling tales
To a child Dhrutarashtra
Abhimanyu's death
Sacrifice of Bhim's son
Durjodhan's swimming on his son's corpse
Child Krishna's varied plays
But nothing about what Krishna told Arjuna
In that battlefield of Kurukshetra.
Maybe she thought
That untold words were too much
To be placed in the story for a child.
A child's instinct
Always tries, strives to get its own philosophy.
She was not a philosopher
Lived her life in a boundary, served all of us
Without being asked how she was!!!
Our cries and demands were so much
That we never tried to listen to her heart
Suppressed and unblossomed
She passed away
And now a star in the sky

Visible at night.
Whenever I go to bed
I call her and ask her
Grandma!
How are you in heaven?
You must be playing with the Sun or the Moon
As I was with you.
Does it rain there?
Does winter come?
Remember Grandmaa, remember that evening
A downpour
And I sitting nearby
Hearing the story of Uddalaka
A great devotee
That I may not be
Remember that little sparrow
It was struggling in that heavy rain
We were the spectators of its ups and downs
Remember I asked you
Why didn't the sparrow call Lord Krishna for help?
And you said that it was a bird, it could not pronounce
Krishna's name, then I stood up to help the sparrow
But you would not let me go
Do you meet that sparrow in heaven?
Or sparrows cannot go to heaven?
She only gives a smile
And vanishes.

2. My Grandpa and Grandma

My grandpa and grandma
The superlative of pa and ma
One knows who Sita's father is
The other one does not know who Bharat's mother is
I want to go now
I don't want to listen to you
Go go, don't tell me later
Shut your mouth and go away!!
Countering every minute
War between yes and no
Pride and prejudice
Abhimaan and Abhimanini
Pa and Ma witness
As they will enact a play tomorrow!!!

3. My Granny Had a Fairy

My granny had a fairy
She wore a white attire
Held a magic stick
Flew in the air
Bright was her arrival
Dark was the time
Love was her duty
Nature was so fair
My granny told me
Heaven was her home
She was not for tomb
I could see her
When I was on my granny's lap
I used to meet her in my dream
To share with her all my scream!!!

4. My Granny's Ghost

In my granny's words

A ghost is not normal

Huge teeth, huge eyes

Nail can be of one kilometer

Nose is equal to a garden

A mountainous one

Is the figure of a ghost

But I have only heard

About female ghost

My granny never tells about male ghost!!

Frightening ferocious

Blood Tears

Revenge murder

Cruel wizard

Oh! What a story of horror!!!

5. My Grandma's Tears

My parents always introduce me to my grandma

As if I am unknown to her

They don't know that

She is my source of smile

She is my beacon- light

She is my philosopher and guide!

She sings to me

What a music! I fall asleep.

My parents don't know that

What tears me?

It is nothing but my granny's tears.

Sometimes, I find dried drops

In a dry land, oh fragile weakness

Non-sticky time

What a life is this!!

Only mime and mime!

6. Words

Each word has a life
It comes and goes away
As a man, as a flower, as a bird
Do you remember the number?
The more the number,
The more you walk away.
Just voice a word, and the word will tell you
Who you are?
Just voice a word, and the word will tell you
Where you are?
Words have tongues, eyes and ears
Oh! Yes
They have forms also
To shape you and to save you!!!

7. Will You Come Back, My Son?

Will you come back, my son?
Will you come back in this Phagun
Forgetting the tear, the blow and the gun?
It is heard that you are killing
But unheard that you are already killed
You will be raised, after the black night
Defeating the Dragons inside and outside
As the resurrection goes on......
Still I can see a bag hanging on the wall
Some homework yet to be done
O my son!!
Where have you gone?
Remembering you, her heart was beating
For the months, she cried the time you left
Sitting near by the window
Looking for you, she passed away
Her eyes were waiting for a blink
During your birthday
But the cuckoo never sang in her heart
In Spring also....

Some of your friends are well-named now
I see their children going to school
They have been told that you are a demon
And I am watching them sucking and sucked
Had you been told and guarded
I would have had my grand-children now
Who could not have been told about any demon......
My son! My soul!
Where have you gone?

8. Sisyphus

Not a Myth,
But a timeless apotheosis of existence
Cursed for years uncountable
Though we are numbered somewhere
And explored
The meaning of meaninglessness
That gods are afraid of,
An obscurity
That no man of thoughts and knowledge
Can understand,
Silent, strong and stout
In front of the Universe to guide us
How to sit still?
How not to condition our minds?
How not to be a slave of desires but a master of living!!!

9. I Doubt

I doubt my 'self 'and the self of the World
Born as a stranger, die as no one being in someone
I desire, I shout I strife
Though I know all my acts are futile
So pompous so beautiful so intelligent we are
For a burial in the graveyard……………………..
The question is certain but the answer is not
So I don't know WHO am I?
My quest is endless
But my bone is earthy
I doubt the INFINITY
While standing on the soil
Think this World is not only for the Journey of Eternity!!!

10. Smoke

Smoke in the sky
A sudden pathetic cry
Where is the city!
Where are the people!
Scattered ......
In blood, bone and in bombs!!!
Still there is a Moon
Out of the smoke
Maybe a Sun rising tomorrow.
You will go for a walk
Maybe not on the same road
To have a smoke somewhere
You may get voices
Moaning for the babies
Men and women, young and old
Under the same Sun or the same Moon.
Behold this field
Look at every walker, every sitter, and every runner
So indifferent to the voices
Just consoling
For the unknown, unwilled
Martyrs of that night

In village or in city
In Mumbai or in New York
Someone unknown or known
There is always a fear of smoke
I am afraid of seeing you on the road
You must have told your wife
That you would go for shopping together
You must have told your son
That you would drop him to his school today
And you don't know where the next smoke is.
There is a burning within
You and your friends or foes
Known or unknown
To burn and also to be burned
For a smoke somewhere
With a belief of alluring purgatorio
Though it is difficult to see in smoke
Who stands there?
Satan or God!!!

11. A Shadow

Wherever we go
A shadow follows us
From birth to death.
It passes through shadows
In this World of possibilities
Always countering
Always becoming.
I have never seen it
Crying, smiling, desiring
Loving, pretending, speaking
As its friends do.
Not only with me
With you, with him or her or them
It was and it will be......
Though the shadows can be caught
The shadow is out of time's clutches.
From morn to eve
It weaves the net
To follow each shadow's step
Till the last horizon comes
Where the Sun never sets
Where it declares, "what follows you when you arrive

The same follows you when you depart!!!"

12. Crucifixion Goes on...

Our Days, Our moments and our meetings
Last in us till we last
The sky is so vast
This World changes so fast
Hope for an immortal mark as Tithonus
Is nothing but an illusion that lasts...............
A bird sings differently
By asking itself a question
Why all are indifferent,
O World! O people!
Could you hear Jesus' last words?
He is a genuine father
How could he react if you crucify him?
It's like a child stabbing thorn to its father
And father only laughs, and says
You are a child; you don't know what you do.
This life is nothing but a child's game
We are nothing but children
He is the only the absolute rational human
What a time is this!
Each moment we crucify a noble thought
Crucifixion goes on, Kurukhetra repeats

The World around sees it being a mere spectator
Infinite no of plays we have, we have infinite no of spectators
But the tragedy is few are the actors
Absorbed in our filthy affairs
Feel proud by performing a worldly act
Ignoring His voice childishly we spend a noble life.
What we get at last?
A name written on our tomb
That can be destroyed by any storm!!!

13. Under that Mountain

Under that mountain
There was a tree
Under that tree
There was a cottage
Where stories were heard
About the mountain, tree and cottage
In one winter evening
I saw a lantern
I heard words
About many unheard unknown worlds
The more I stayed there, the more I knew
About them, old and new!!
When I go there now,
I find a multi-cuisine Restaurant
Though the old is white, painted evergreen
The new looks at it, as if stands a king or queen.
I could see a mountain on its wall
To remind the visitors
Of the bygone era
They come and go
They eat, drink, smoke and do mazaa
They gossip and do masti and order pizza

The mountain is buried, its dew in a bottle
I can get mango throughout the year
No need of Spring or Summer
My mobile can welcome cuckoo any time!
Oh! There is a cottage
Barnished and polished
Where air is conditioned
Water is processed
For a fountain musical
Far from the natural whimsical
A fashion to feel like the one
Where the grasshopper does not sing
And grass is on a green carpet!!!

14. Come Online, Dear!

Come online, dear!

I am in a net-cafe

Thousands go to bed together

Without touching one another

If words on a screen can bleed....can fall tear

Then I miss you....I like you

Where are you ?

Could we meet one day

Under a tree, nearby some park

With a symposium of dates, romance and all that

We don't know each other but we trust

Such trust is betrayed, not everywhere

I have read in today's newspaper

It was a thorny day for someone

Deceived by words is so easy

Isn't it my dear?

Oh! There is always a power

I have to sign out and switch off

I have to bid farewell

But I will sms you anytime

Don't forget to dial my number

It is from zero to nine

Not different from you
Romeo died because Juliet couldn't sms
Othello suspects because Desdemona couldn't sms
So unfortunate they were
They did not have this alluring device.